I0566514

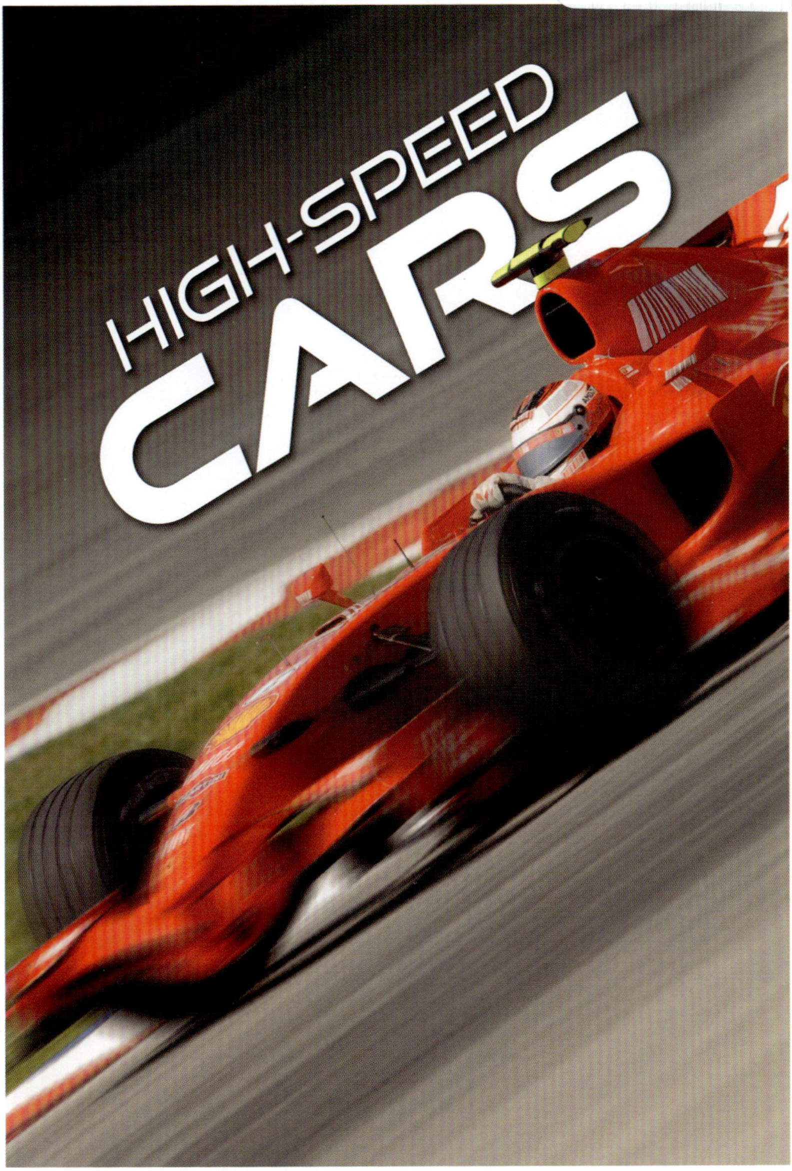

HIGH-SPEED CARS

Heather E. Schwartz

Consultants

Jeremy Kinney
Associate Director of Research, Collections,
and Curatorial Affairs
National Air and Space Museum

Cheryl Lane, M.Ed.
Seventh Grade Science Teacher
Chino Valley Unified School District

Michelle Wertman, M.S.Ed.
Literacy Specialist
New York City Public Schools

Publishing Credits

Rachelle Cracchiolo, M.S.Ed., *Publisher*
Emily R. Smith, M.A.Ed., *SVP of Content Development*
Véronique Bos, *VP of Creative*
Dani Neiley, *Editor*
Robin Erickson, *Senior Art Director*
Kevin Pham, *Senior Graphic Designer*
Jill Malcolm, *Senior Graphic Designer*

Smithsonian Enterprises

Avery Naughton, *Licensing Coordinator*
Paige Towler, *Editorial Lead*
Jill Corcoran, *Senior Director, Licensed Publishing*
Brigid Ferraro, *Vice President of New Business and Licensing*
Carol LeBlanc, *President*

Image Credits: p.4 (middle) Shutterstock/Jack Skeens; p.4 (bottom) Shutterstock/Brandon Woyshnis; p.5 Alamy/Marc Hill; p.6 (middle) Library of Congress [LC-USZ62-89691]; p.6 (bottom) Alamy/Dmitry Orlov; p.7 Getty Images/Gamma-Keystone; p.8 (middle) Getty Images; p.8 (bottom) Getty Images/Sports Illustrated; p.9 Shutterstock/Todamo; p.16 Shutterstock/Ev. Safronov; p.17 Shutterstock/Oen Michael; p.18 Shutterstock/Grindstone Media Group; p.19 (bottom) Shutterstock/Sue Thatcher; p.20 Shutterstock/1933 Media Productions; p.21 (middle) Shutterstock/Big Blink Creative; p.22 Shutterstock/David Acosta Allely; p.23 Shutterstock/Grindstone Media Group; p.25 (top) Shutterstock/adolf martinez soler; p.25 (bottom) Shutterstock/Oasishifi; p.27 (top) Shutterstock/Sport car hub; p.27 (middle) Shutterstock/AlessioDeMarco; p.27 (bottom) Shutterstock/lev radin; p.32 Shutterstock/Roman Belogorodov; all other images from Shutterstock and/or iStock

Library of Congress Cataloging in Publication Control Number: 2024033335

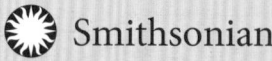
Smithsonian

TCM | Teacher Created Materials

© 2025 Smithsonian Institution. The name "Smithsonian" and the Smithsonian logo are registered trademarks owned by the Smithsonian Institution.

This book may not be reproduced or distributed in any way without prior written consent from the publisher.

5482 Argosy Avenue
Huntington Beach, CA 92649
www.tcmpub.com
ISBN 979-8-7659-6878-9
© 2025 Teacher Created Materials, Inc.
Printed by: 51497
Printed in: China

Table of Contents

Speed Is Spectacular

All kinds of cars zip through the streets. They are also parked in parking lots, on driveways, and on side streets. They're such a common part of our everyday world that we hardly notice them. But when they go superfast, we can't look away!

High-speed cars attract attention whether they are on the road or on a racetrack. The bodies of these cars draw our eyes because they're different from ordinary cars. Their shapes aren't quite the same as the standard cars most people use. Plus, when these cars are on regular roads, driving the **speed limit**, they have the potential for more.

When high-speed cars take off on a racetrack, their speed is astonishing. Race cars seem to fly by as they battle full force for the lead position. It's easy to tell from the sounds they make that their engines are built differently under the **hood**. Ordinary cars can't be driven in the same way as high-speed cars. And until recently, even cars built for racing couldn't hit the astounding speeds they reach today.

The history of high-speed cars starts with the invention of the first modern **vehicle**. With continuing technological advances and record-shattering races, there is no finish line in sight!

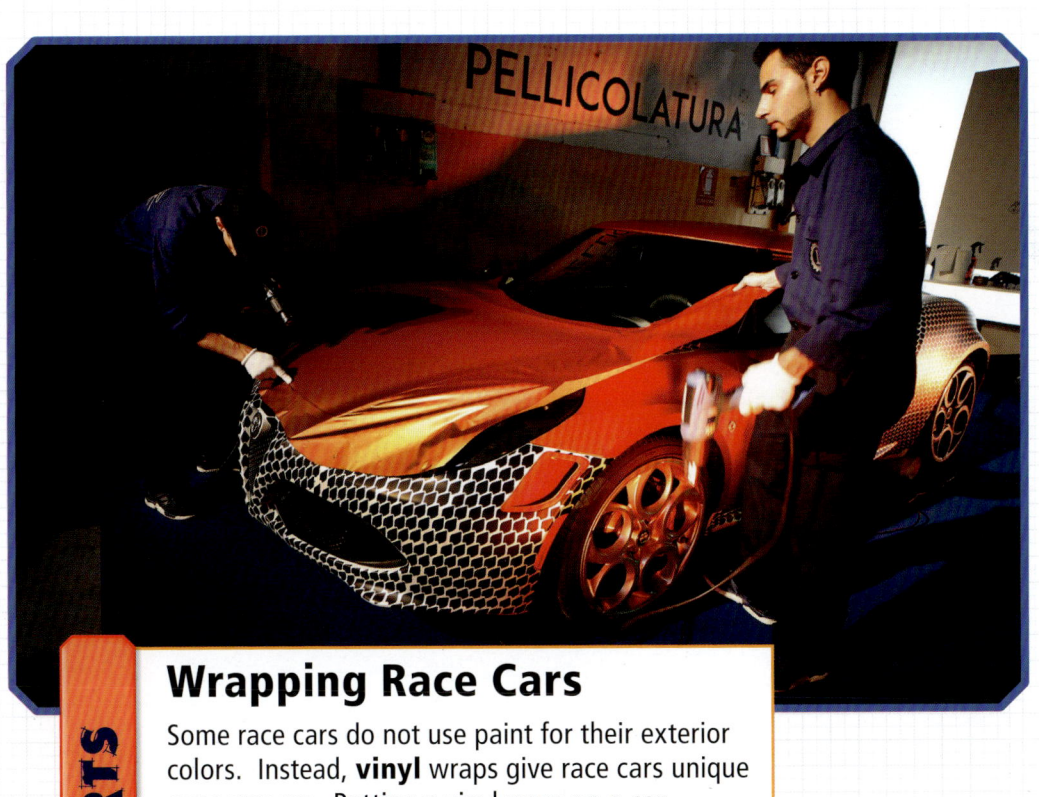

ARTS

Wrapping Race Cars

Some race cars do not use paint for their exterior colors. Instead, **vinyl** wraps give race cars unique appearances. Putting a vinyl wrap on a car involves applying a large sheet of vinyl like a big sticker to the body of a car. These wraps can have special designs and unique, **iridescent** colors.

High-Speed History

Before cars were invented, people used horse-drawn carriages to get around their cities and towns. But this type of transportation was slow and inefficient. People wanted to invent new vehicles that would help them travel to and from places more quickly.

In 1886, an engineer named Karl Benz created a new kind of vehicle. He hit the streets of Germany with the first modern car. His car was powered by an **internal combustion engine** that ran on gasoline. Benz had built on other inventors' ideas, but he was the first person to put the engine to work in a car. This allowed the car to reach a top speed of 16 kilometers (10 miles) per hour.

Benz's 1886 car

Other inventors saw the potential in Benz's car and began to work on improving the design. They wanted to make cars that would go faster. By 1894, drivers had begun to race their cars and hit new top speeds. In 1895, the first real car race took place in France. The winner reached an **average** speed of 24 km (15 mi.) per hour. At the time, this vehicle was considered a high-speed car.

By 1900, race cars could go nearly 48 km (30 mi.) per hour. These cars were raced on roads that were designed for horse and wagon traffic and not for cars. This made car racing especially dangerous.

The Paris–Bordeaux–Paris Trail race of June 1895 was the first car race.

Further Developments

In 1911, the first Indianapolis 500 took place. This U.S. car race happened at the Indianapolis Motor Speedway, which had a track for testing cars. In this race, high-speed cars reached nearly 120 km (75 mi.) per hour. Over the next 60 years, these high speeds more than doubled. By the late 1970s, cars that raced in the Indianapolis 500 were hitting close to 260 km (161 mi.) per hour. That is much too fast for regular roads and highways.

Indianapolis 500 in 1911

Indianapolis 500 in 1978

Driving at high speeds and winning races have always required a lot of skill. But drivers weren't the only ones in charge when it came to how fast their cars could go. Companies started building race cars with speed in mind every step of the way. They thought about **velocity** when they built the engines. They designed car bodies to move forward with ease.

Race cars weren't the only high-speed cars in development. Hypercars, the highest performance and most expensive high-speed cars, were also in the works. **Luxury carmakers** began building these cars to be legal to drive on racetracks—*and* on regular roads! In 1987, the Ferrari F40 had a top speed of 323 km (201 mi.) per hour. In 1993, the McLaren F1 hit 386 km (240 mi.) per hour. That record was broken in the early 2000s. And every year since, carmakers have continued to build new cars, testing the limits of speed.

FUN FACT

Carmakers around the world build high-speed cars. For example, Ferrari is based in Italy. McLaren Automotive is based in England. These luxury brands—and many others—are well-known throughout the car industry.

Ferrari factory in Italy

Car Features

High-speed cars are powered by internal combustion engines that use gasoline as fuel. Complex parts and pieces work together to move these cars. And different features, such as wheels and tires, set high-speed cars apart from regular cars.

Inside an Engine

Starting a car begins with the **ignition** system. First, a driver has to insert and turn a key or push a button to turn on a car. This triggers the ignition switch to take power from the car's battery. Power from the battery travels through wires to the ignition coil, which sends the power into the spark plugs. Spark plugs are connected to the car's engine.

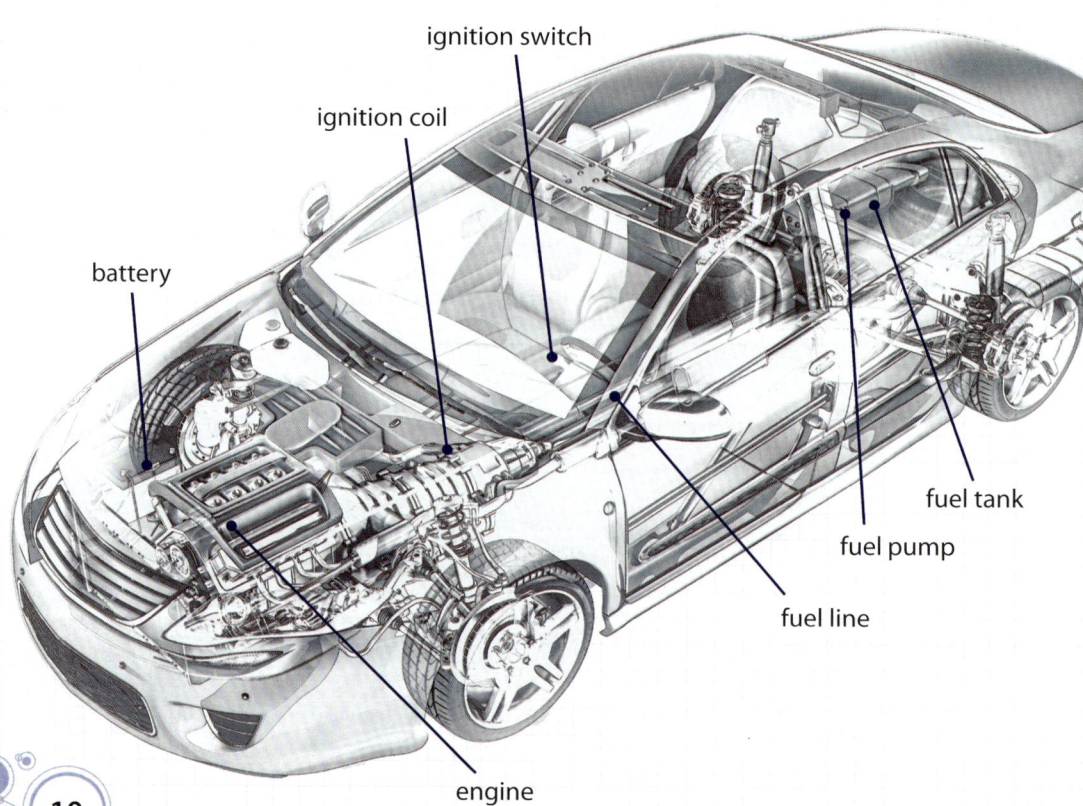

ignition switch

ignition coil

battery

fuel tank

fuel pump

fuel line

engine

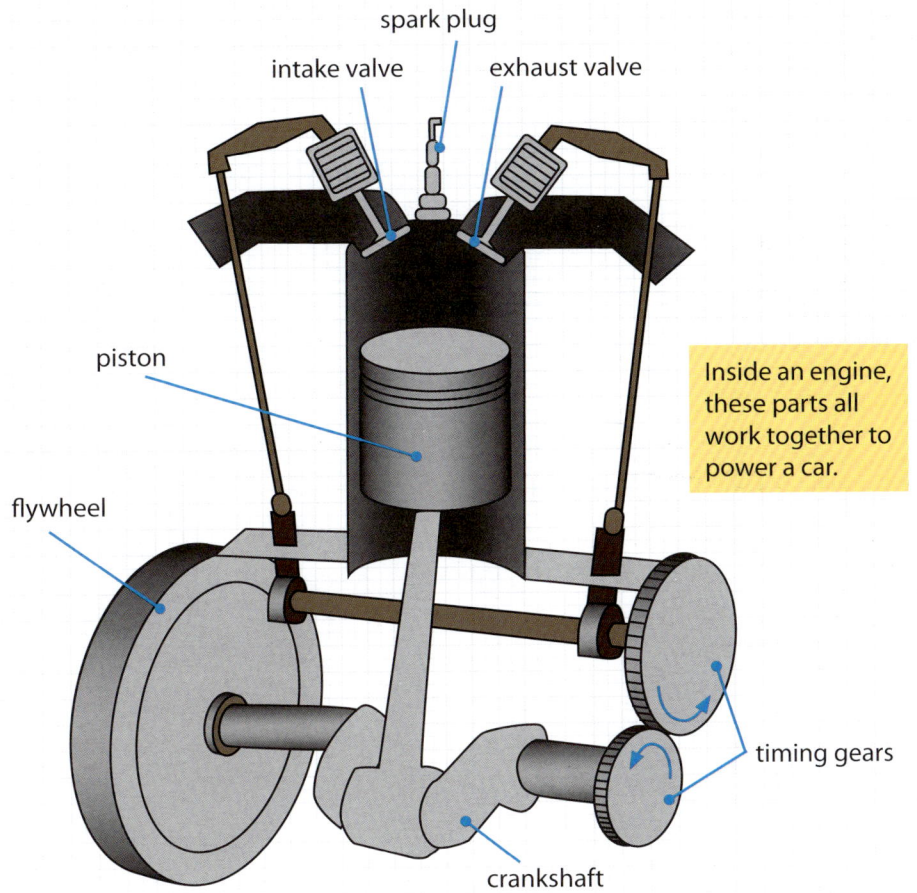

spark plug

intake valve   exhaust valve

piston

Inside an engine, these parts all work together to power a car.

flywheel

timing gears

crankshaft

At the same time, the ignition switch also turns on the car's fuel pump. This pump moves gasoline, or fuel, from the car's fuel tank through the fuel line. After traveling through the intake valve, the fuel ends up in the engine, where it blends with air. Spark plugs, which are taking power from the car's battery, ignite this mixture. This causes a sequence of small explosions called *combustion* within the engine's **cylinders**. Combustion is a chemical reaction between substances that creates heat and light. Finally, heat energy from combustion causes moving parts called *pistons* to move up and down inside the cylinders. As the fuel burns, it releases **exhaust** through the exhaust valve. The exhaust is expelled from the car through a tailpipe.

Mechanical Energy

As pistons move up and down, they transform heat energy into mechanical energy. Mechanical energy is what makes a car move. Mechanical energy is a combination of potential energy and kinetic energy, or the energy of motion. This energy makes a car's moving parts work.

Inside a car's engine, the pistons are connected to a zigzag part called a *crankshaft*. The movement of the pistons causes the crankshaft and timing gears to turn in circles. The crankshaft changes the up-and-down movement of energy from the pistons into a rotational motion.

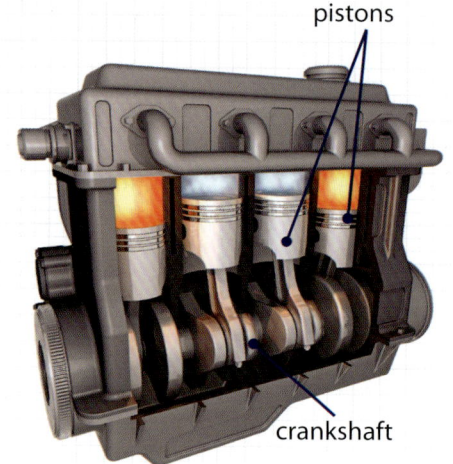

pistons

crankshaft

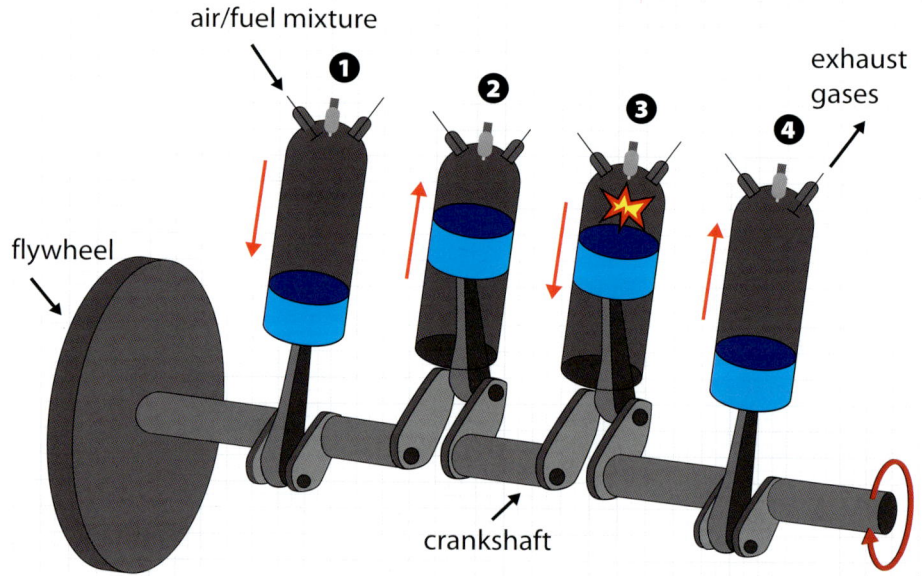

air/fuel mixture

exhaust gases

flywheel

crankshaft

❶ Air and fuel mixture goes in.
❷ Intake valve closes and piston moves up.
❸ The spark plug ignites the air/fuel mixture.
❹ The piston moves up and exhaust is pushed out.

The crankshaft is connected to a disc-shaped part that also turns. In some cars, this is called a *flywheel*. In other cars, it is called a *flexplate*. This part stores mechanical energy to keep the engine running once the car is turned on. And when a driver steps on the gas pedal of a car, the flywheel or flexplate transfers energy through several more parts to the car's wheels. This energy makes the wheels rotate, putting the car in motion.

Wheels and Tires

Wheels are the shiny, metal circles that you see on a car. Rubber tires are attached around a car's wheels. Tires are inflated with air to make a car drive smoothly and to absorb impact from bumps along a road. Tires also provide **traction** while a car is on the road so the driver has control of the vehicle. When a driver steps on the brake pedal of a car, brakes are applied to the wheel. The car will begin to slow down or fully stop as the tires create friction with the road. Friction is a force that resists motion and slows down objects.

Many different types of tires can be put onto a car's wheels.

Special High-Speed Features

You'd have a hard time hitting top racing speeds in a regular road car. That's because the engines and tires of race cars are built differently.

Cars built for racing need engines with exceptional power. While most regular cars have four or six cylinders in their engines, some cars that are built to compete have eight. These engines are called *V8 engines* because the cylinders are arranged in a V shape. With extra cylinders comes extra pistons, meaning that these race cars can create more energy faster than regular cars. The extra pistons mean that they can **accelerate** faster, too.

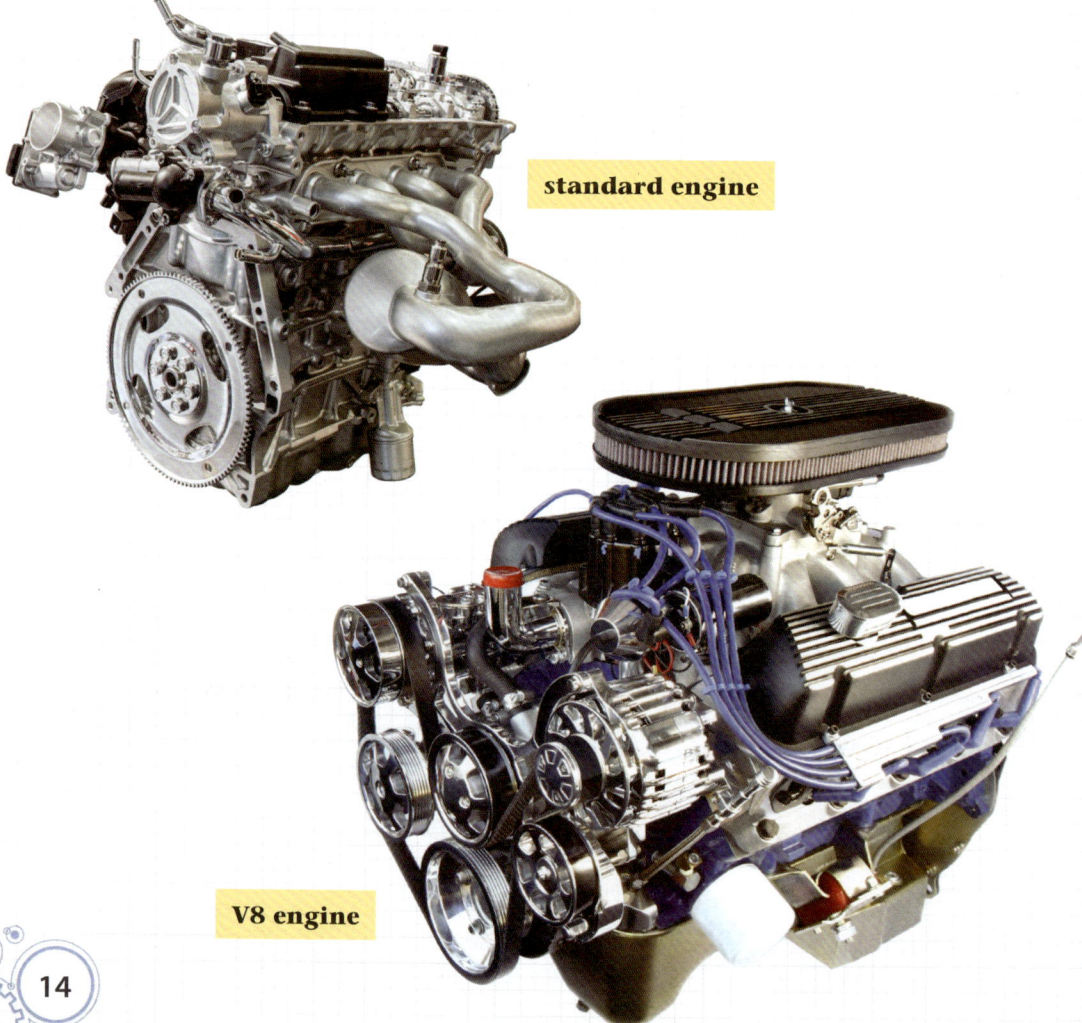

standard engine

V8 engine

Have you ever looked at a regular car tire? You'll notice that the surface has **tread** and grooves in it. These markings allow rain and snow on the ground to move through so that the tire can have stable contact with the road. This is a similar concept to the tread in hiking shoes. A grooved and patterned surface allows for traction and stability.

When you look at race car tires, you'll notice that the surface is smooth and wide. Drivers mostly race in dry weather conditions so they don't need tread. With a smooth surface, a race car tire has more surface area in contact with the road. These tires grip a dry road better than a regular grooved tire. This way, a driver has more control when speeding up and racing through turns on a track.

race car tires

rearview mirror

FUN FACT

Rearview mirrors are flat mirrors attached to the interior ceiling of a car. They allow a driver to see the road and vehicles behind them. The first person to use a rearview mirror was the race car driver who won the first Indianapolis 500 race in 1911. By 1921, rearview mirrors were being made to put in regular cars.

Built for Speed

Regular road cars are built with stability in mind, and they are meant to last for years. Race cars, on the other hand, are built for speed. Their parts are pushed to the limit during races. And if parts wear out or break, specially trained mechanics can fix and rebuild these cars for the next race.

The overall structure of race cars is very important. These cars have strong but lightweight frames. Engines, wheels, and other mechanical parts are attached to the frames. Race cars are made to have less mass and weight than regular road cars. Mass is the total amount of matter in an object, while weight is the force of gravity on an object.

Engineers work on a car's brakes during a race.

Engineers use computer systems that link to a car's sensors to run tests and check the condition of certain parts.

Race Car Engineers

Race car engineers are critical to a car's success on the track. They analyze data from sensors inside a car. The sensors show information about tire temperature, friction between parts, the balance of a car, and more. Engineers use this information, along with math and physics, to make adjustments. Engineers help keep drivers safe and get race cars moving faster.

When race cars are built to be lightweight, they can move faster than regular cars. Force, mass, and acceleration work together to propel these cars forward. Force is created when a driver turns on a car and presses the gas pedal. This gets the engine working, which makes the car move. The lightweight mass of a race car means it accelerates faster than a heavy car with more mass. Skilled race car drivers know how to use the right amount of force when accelerating and braking. They make it look easy, but driving a race car efficiently takes a lot of hard work!

More Than Meets the Eye

Race cars move differently from road cars, and they look different, too. Race car bodies often have distinct and flashy styles. But they are not designed that way for appearance alone. The shapes of race cars help them battle against air resistance, or drag. This force is the enemy of speed.

Here's how air resistance works. When a high-speed car races around a track, it pushes through the air to move forward. This creates friction between the car and the air, ultimately slowing down the car. Every car that races will encounter air resistance—it is an unavoidable reality in racing.

SCIENCE

Working Together

One racing strategy is called *drafting*. This involves one car following closely behind another car. The lead car blocks air from moving, creating air pressure that pulls the second car forward. The second car reduces the air resistance for the lead car. The result is that both cars gain speed!

To lessen the effects of air resistance, race cars are designed to be **aerodynamic**. Their streamlined shapes decrease air resistance. Their shapes also create **downforce**, which keeps the race cars firmly on the ground and allows them to take corners faster and gain more speed.

Many extra parts help a high-speed car outpace the competition. These parts direct how air flows around a car, lowering air resistance. A curved part called a *splitter* sits on the front bumper. Thin, ridged dive planes are on the left and right sides of the front bumper. Side skirts are long, thin pieces that attach near the bottoms of the doors. Finally, a rear wing connects to the back of a car. Carmakers build their race cars with these different parts and adjust them as needed to improve speed.

A mechanical engineer reviews the results of an aerodynamic test.

rear wing

splitter

dive plane

side skirt

Racing to the Top

Now that we've learned about the features, forces, and designs of high-speed cars, let's zoom through some examples of these cars operating in our modern world.

Breaking Records

In 2019, the luxury carmaker Bugatti wanted to know how fast their Bugatti Chiron could go. This luxury hypercar had a long, low body that was made to slice through the air with precision. The engine could accelerate from 0 to 100 km (0 to 62 mi.) per hour in just over 2 seconds. Could it possibly beat a speed barrier no car had broken before?

Bugatti set up a test with their Chiron Super Sport car. Driver Andy Wallace wore a helmet and a fire suit. He was strapped into the car with a special harness for added safety. As he sped along a test track, in mere seconds, the car reached 322 km (200 mi.) per hour. The speedometer kept climbing. Within one minute, the record was broken. The car went over 483 km (300 mi.) per hour. It was the first vehicle in the world to do so! It topped out at 490.5 km (304.7 mi.) per hour.

Bugatti Chiron Super Sport

Measuring Speed

Every car has a speedometer, which is a tool that measures speed. Many modern cars have digital speedometers. They display speed on a digital screen on the dashboard. Special sensors inside a car measure the rotation of the wheels, which is then converted to speed.

SSC Tuatara

In 2020, a hypercar company called *SSC* claimed to have broken that record. Parts of their Tuatara car's body were inspired by jet fighter planes. They claimed that the Tuatara reached a speed of 533 km (331 mi.) per hour! But in 2021, the company confessed that their reported high speed was inaccurate. While the Tuatara was fast, there was no proof that it could outpace the Bugatti.

Modern Race Cars

Hypercars may battle for top speed records, but race cars are made for one reason: to prove how fast they can go on a track! Modern race cars show their stuff in competitions that draw fans from all over the world.

The Indianapolis 500 has been held every year since 1911. Specially made Indy cars compete in this race. Indy cars are single-seat race cars with open **cockpits** and open wheels. In 2022, the winner sped around the track at more than double the speed of the racers in the 1911 race!

Formula One racing is the highest level of international car racing. Formula One cars are similar to Indy cars, but they are the fastest **regulated** racing cars in the world. In 2005, a driver named Juan Pablo Montoya set a record for the highest top speed in a Formula One race. He hit 372.6 km (231.5 mi.) per hour!

Juan Pablo Montoya

In stock car races, stock cars compete on oval tracks to see who can complete laps the fastest. Stock cars are regular road cars with specific changes that increase their speed. These cars are typically heavier than Formula One cars. At the Daytona International Speedway, a racetrack in Florida, stock cars compete in the Daytona 500. As of 2023, the fastest race ever recorded belongs to a driver named Buddy Baker. He won the race in 1980. His average speed was 285.8 km (177.6 mi.) per hour.

Daytona International Speedway

Many Ways to Win

Crossing the finish line first isn't the only way to win in car racing. Statistics measure other victories, too. For example, drivers set and break records for the number of laps they make in the lead position during races. Averages are used to calculate which cars had the top finishing positions throughout a racing season.

MATHEMATICS

Looking Ahead

Since their invention, cars have gotten much faster on both roads and racetracks. But what does the future hold? Will cars continue to gain speed, and if so, how?

One recent change in car design is happening in the engine. Hybrid cars run on a combination of gasoline and electricity. Less gasoline creates less exhaust, which is good for the environment. Plus, this combo can boost acceleration at the same time. Hybrid race cars have smaller, lighter engines. These engines allow them to have less mass, helping them accelerate faster.

Modern carmakers experiment with different materials to build high-speed car bodies. They work with lighter materials, such as carbon fiber, to make cars less heavy. They also tap into technology that wasn't around in the past. Special 3D printers can be used to create new lightweight parts. Special computer software and **artificial intelligence** are also used to learn how to improve a car's aerodynamics.

Thanks to technology, race car drivers have new ways to practice their skills. Drivers can use virtual reality simulators to experience cars and conditions before big races. This way, when they hit the track, they're better prepared to push the limits.

FUN FACT

What will racing look like in 2050? A tech company that is working with Formula One has some ideas. For starters, they want to use artificial intelligence copilots. They also want to create tires that can repair themselves if they get holes.

During races, tires are replaced by pit crews.

The Toyota TS050 Hybrid race car has a V6 engine and an electric battery system.

New engine prototypes can be created with 3D printers.

virtual reality simulator

An Even Faster Future

Engines roar as race cars speed through a race's last turn and accelerate toward the finish line. In the stands, fans clap and yell, rooting for their favorite drivers to pull ahead of the pack. The deciding factor in determining the winner all comes down to speed. Which car and driver will handle the track best today?

Speed is a rate of movement that can be measured, marveled over, and appreciated. It only makes sense that carmakers and racing fans alike want to see just how fast high-speed cars can go. Yet each time a speed record is broken, a new goal is set. Carmakers go back to work while fans wait in anticipation. Everyone is eager to find out whether an even faster high-speed car is possible.

With modern advancements and technology, it seems likely that this cycle will continue. Fans will keep clamoring for more impressive speeds. Carmakers will continue to create better engines and more aerodynamic designs. And high-speed cars will break increasingly faster records as we move into the future.

Electric battery systems like this one may become more common in the future.

McLaren 720S
Spider hypercar

Formula 1 race

Formula E race
for electric cars

STEAM CHALLENGE

Define the Problem

Autonomous, or self-driving, vehicles are becoming more common. Carmakers are trying to reduce the amount of gas and electric energy these cars use. Engineers are seeking to build lightweight vehicles that minimize friction from the air and ground to conserve energy. They have asked for your help to design two autonomous car models. Then, you will choose one to build and test.

Constraints: You can only use the materials that are provided. You may only test your car on the approved ramp.

Criteria: Your car should roll down the ramp as quickly as possible and weigh the least amount.

Research and Brainstorm

How does mass affect kinetic energy? How are mass, kinetic energy, and speed related? How can you build a car that reduces friction while still being safe on the roads?

Design and Build

Sketch at least two designs for your autonomous vehicle. Label the materials you intend to use and how you will assemble your car. Share your ideas with a group. Then, decide which prototype you will build together.

Test and Improve

Once your vehicle is built, weigh it and record the weight. Then, bring your car to the testing ramp. One person places the vehicle at the top of the ramp and releases it. At the same time, one person starts the timer. When the vehicle reaches the end of the ramp, the timer should be stopped. Record your time. What changes can you make to your vehicle to increase the speed? Adjust or rebuild your car as needed. Then, test it again, recording the weight and drive time.

Reflect and Share

What other factors could increase or decrease the amount of kinetic energy in your model? What part of this challenge was most interesting for you? What part of the challenge was the most difficult, and how did you overcome the obstacle?

Glossary

accelerate—to move faster

aerodynamic—having a shape that reduces drag from air moving past

artificial intelligence—the power of a machine to imitate intelligent human behavior

average—a number that expresses the central or typical value in a set of data

cockpits—spaces in vehicles where they are steered

cylinders—tubes in which pistons of an engine move

downforce—a combination of air resistance and gravity that pushes a car toward the ground

exhaust—waste gases expelled from an engine

hood—a cover over the engine of a vehicle

ignition—a device used to ignite the fuel mixture in a gasoline engine

internal combustion engine—an engine in which the fuel is burned within engine cylinders

iridescent—shimmery colors that change when seen from different angles

luxury carmakers—carmakers who build expensive, high-quality cars with advanced features

pistons—sliding pieces that move inside cylinders

regulated—controlled through rules or laws

speed limit—the maximum speed a vehicle can travel along a road

traction—the grip of a tire on a road

tread—the thick molded part of a vehicle tire that grips the road

vehicle—a machine used for transporting people or goods, such as a car or truck

velocity—the speed of something in a given direction

vinyl—human-made resin or plastic that is used for wallpapers and other covering materials, such as decals and stickers

Index

Nissan 370Z

Do you want to work with cars?

Here are some tips to keep in mind for the future.

"Take what you are learning about engineering and technology in school, experiment with those ideas, and apply your experience to building your own fast-moving vehicles, whether they be models, remote-control cars, or, when you get older, full-size automobiles."

– Jeremy Kinney, Associate Director of Research, Collections, and Curatorial Affairs, National Air and Space Museum

"There's always room for improvement in cars and users are often the best inventors. Keep your ideas in a notebook and send ideas to manufacturers or explore patenting them yourself."

– Kathleen Franz, Chair and Curator, Division of Work & Industry, National Museum of American History